Puss in Books

Puss in Books

Our best-loved writers on their best-loved cats

by

Paul Magrs

HarperCollins*Publishers*

HarperCollins*Publishers*
1 London Bridge Street
London SE1 9GF

www.harpercollins.co.uk

HarperCollins*Publishers*
1st Floor, Watermarque Building, Ringsend Road
Dublin 4, Ireland

First published by HarperCollins*Publishers* 2023

3 5 7 9 10 8 6 4 2

A catalogue record of this book is available from the British Library

ISBN 978-0-00-860537-7

Printed and bound in Latvia

MIX
Paper | Supporting
responsible forestry
FSC™ C007454

This book is produced from independently certified FSC™ paper to ensure
responsible forest management.

For more information visit: www.harpercollins.co.uk/green

for

fester Cat

and

Bernard Socks

Hellooo! This is a book of drawings of all kinds of cats by Paul Magrs. Here you'll find cats in many different moods and attitudes. Dozing or dashing or having a mooch about. Cats having adventures on the page.

Winding through the pages there are quotes from literary heroes. There are lines both profound and whimsical. All of them are people trying to pin down exactly what cats have meant to them. Their thoughts are funny, illuminating and sometimes ...

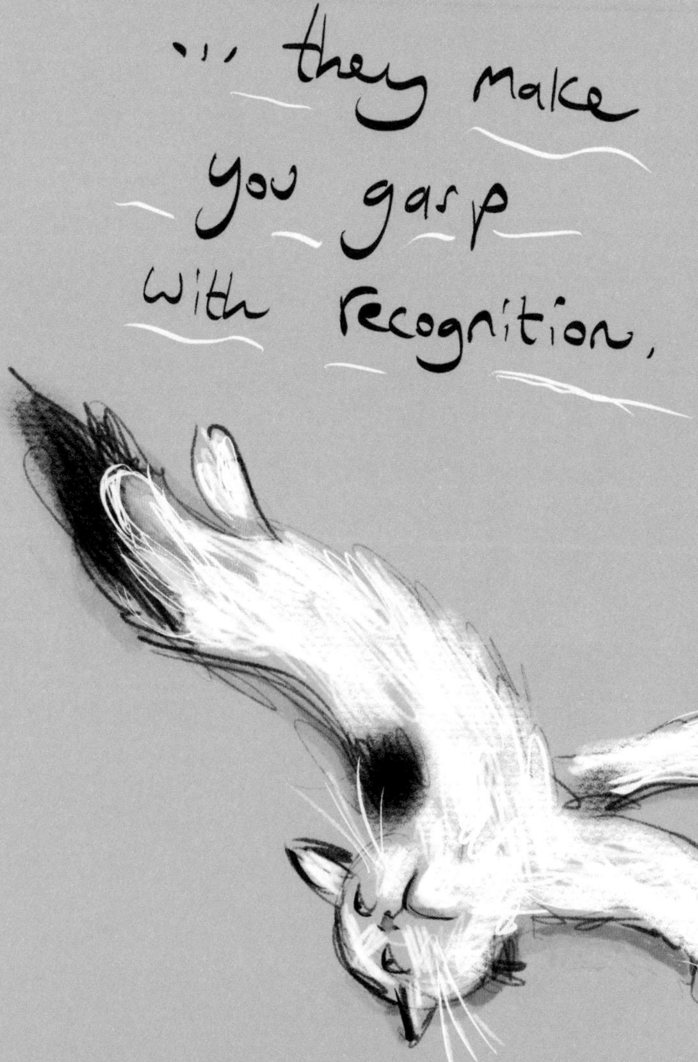
... they make
you gasp
with recognition,

So many writers down the years have been obsessed with cats. There's a real affinity between both species of snarky, selfish, watchful, daydreaming, deeply contemplative, unreliable and changeable creatures.

Many of the cats who've volunteered to feature in this book have been suggested by my extended friendship circle and my social media followers.

"Me, me!"

People seemed keen to have their furry pals take part in this Catalogue of literary felines.

It's the Every - Cat Library.

The higgledy-piggledyness of the quotes and authors is important. I Zig-Zag in my own reading, cutting across genres, following my nose, seeing where each book leads me next.

I suppose that way of mooching and sniffing and walking where I will is all a bit <u>Catlike</u>, too.

In these complicated and troublesome times I'm finding the wisdom of cats and their intuitive grasp on how to be happy a very consoling thing.

To me, cats look like they're reading the most interesting thing in the world...

even when they don't

have a book to hand.

It's a gently humorous book, full of the hard-won wisdom of writers who know all about cats. It might even turn out to be inspirational and heart-warming!

(Here's Tripod, who's missing a leg. "I still get about," he says.)

Chapter One,

Animal Nature

"The fervent lover and the sage austere."

— Charles Baudelaire

"I have got my staff up to five meals a day, but there is still room for improvement."

(Chandler wrote letters in the voice of his cat, Taki.)

"He is still only a whisker away from the wilds."

— Jean Burden

"Way down deep, we're all motivated by the same urges. Cats have the courage

to live by them."
— Jim Davis

"After dark
all cats are
leopards."

— Native American
proverb

"Through all this horror my cat stalked unperturbed. Once I saw him perched atop a mountain of bones, and wondered at the secrets that might lie behind his yellow eyes."

—H.P. Lovecraft

"The cats only think about eating fish all day, and don't care about the mice running about."

— Lu You

"Cats are autocrats of naked self-interest."

-Camille Paglia

"Did St Francis preach to the birds? Whatever for? If he really liked

birds he would have done better to preach to the cats."
— Rebecca West

"I am as vigilant as a cat to steal cream."

— William Shakespeare

"I take care of my flowers and my cats, and enjoy food.

And that's living."

—ursula andress

Bruce the Batcat had half a lung removed, but still goes out catching mice.

Chapter Two.

Fun.

"We have our smiles, as it were, painted on."

— Angela Carter

"Your body is not a temple, it's

an amusement park. Enjoy the ride."
— Anthony Bourdain

"It always gives me a shiver when I see a cat

seeing what I can't see."
— Eleanor Farjeon

"God made the cat to give man the pleasure of stroking a tiger."

— françois Joseph Méry

Getting any work done today looks nigh on impossible. Behave, guys.

"Books. Cats. Life is good."

— Edward Gorey

Greta when she was going through her pole-dancing phase...

"Cats never strike a pose that isn't photogenic."

— Lilian Jackson Braun

"Cats are intended to teach us that not everything in Nature has a function."
— Garrison Keillor

Ziggy having a good old sniff of Maxi's bum.

"The only thing a cat worries about is what's happening right now..."

— Lloyd Alexander

"Cities, like cats, will reveal themselves at night."

— Rupert Brooke

We're
off
out.

Chapter Three.

friendship.

"Then it suddenly and dramatically began to clean itself in the way cats do when they want you to know what a big deal you aren't!" — adam REX

"Cats have enormous patience ...

With the limitations of humankind."
— Cleveland Amory

"Cats know how we feel; they just don't give a damn."
— anonymouse

"When I am
feeling
low
all I have
to do is
watch my
cats
and
my

courage
returns."
— Charles Bukowski

"I am one of the most fanatical cat lovers in the business. If you hate them, I might learn to hate you."

— Raymond Chandler

"for every house is incomplete without him."

-Christopher Smart

"I love cats because
I enjoy my home; and
little by little, they become
its visible
soul."
- Jean
Cocteau
*

"Cats know how to obtain food without labour, shelter without confinement, and love

without penalties."
— Walter Lionel George

"Missy is a stealthy cat,
She quietly lies i wait
              for coos and
              kisses,
                    purrs and

              fuss,
They never come too late."
    —Ira Lightman

Jenny's little friend
(on the way to
work)

"I was enchanted by the strangeness of cats."
— Judith Kerr

"What you realise when you've lived with a cat for a long time is that we think we own them, but that's not the way it is.

They simply allow us the pleasure of their company."
— Genki Kawamura

"Cats choose us, we
don't own them."
— Kristen Cast

"When a man loves cats I am his friend and comrade, without further introduction."
— Mark Twain

"Cats regard people as warm-blooded furniture."

— Jacquelyn Mitchard

"I love them, they are so nice and selfish."

— L. M Montgomery

"If I take a walk and I see a cat, I'm happy."
— Haruki Murakami

Haruki Murakami
Kafka on the Shore

"Cats may walk by themselves, but there are times when they need our support."

— Nicholas Dodman

"I and Pangur Bán,
my cat,
'Tis a like task we are
at,

Hunting mice
is his delight,

Hunting words
I sit all night."
— anon

"Help! Help! The Marquis de Carabas is drowning!"

—Charles Perrault

"When my cats aren't happy, I'm not happy."

- Percy Bysshe Shelley

"Authors like cats because they are such quiet, lovable, wise creatures

and cats like authors for the same reasons."
— Robertson Davies

"Are cats strange
animals or do they
so resemble us

that we
find them curious as
we do monkeys?"
— John Steinbeck

"There are few things in life more heartwarming than to be Welcomed by a cat." —Tay Hohoff

"I love my cats, and I guess they think I'm okay."

— Tom Cox

"Time spent with a cat is never wasted."

— Colette

Wishy
Wash

Chapter four.

Philosophy.

"In the eyes of the mouse the cat is a lion."
— Albanian Proverb

"Cats are people, and the sooner the world accepts that fact, the better off the world will be." – H. Allen Smith

"Like all pure creatures, cats are practical."

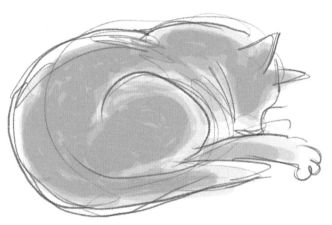

— William S. Burroughs

"Cats are like four-legged poster children for OCD." — Caroline Knapp

"There are no ordinary cats."

Colette

apartment in the Palais-Royal — 1955

"The smallest
feline
is a
masterpiece."
— Leonardo
da Vinci

"I have lived with several Zen masters — all of them Cats."

— Eckhart Tolle

"Cats invented self-esteem. There is not an insecure bone in their body."

— Erma Bombeck

"If cats could write history, their history would be mostly about cats." — Eugen Weber

"Never try to out-stubborn a Cat."

— Robert A. Heinlein

"Guilt isn't in Cat vocabulary."

— Helen Brown

"Human beings, for one reason or another, may hide their feelings, but a cat does not." — Ernest Hemingway

"Could the purr be anything but contemplative?"

—Irving Townsend

"a dog, I have always said, is prose; a cat is a poem."
—Jean Burden

"She don't say much, but you can tell enough to make you anxious not to hear the whole of it."
—Jerome K. Jerome

"Relying on what they can touch, smell and see,

Cats are not ruled by words."

— John N. Gray

"I will do just as you wish," said no cat ever."

—Laini Taylor

"If a fish is the movement of water embodied, given shape, then a cat

is a diagram and pattern of subtle air."
— Doris Lessing

"a dog growls when it's angry and wags its tail when it's pleased.

Now I growl when I'm pleased and wag my tail when I'm angry. Therefore I'm mad." — Lewis Carroll

"Cats are like a little bit 'f heaven on earth, their purring not unlike the stir of angel wings."

-Theresa Mancuso

"Big zucchini, small kitten."
— Marge Piercy

"Dogs own space
    and cats own time."
- Nicola Griffith

"I wish I could write as mysterious as a cat,"

— Edgar Allan Poe

*

"Cats and books are my universe.

Both are infinitely fascinating and full of mystery."

— Rai aren

"A cat improves the garden wall in sunshine, and the hearth in foul weather."

— Judith Merkle Riley

"The effect of a cat on your concentration is remarkable, very mysterious."

— Muriel Spark

"Cats are a very mysterious kind of folk. There is always more passing in their minds than we are aware of."

— Walter Scott

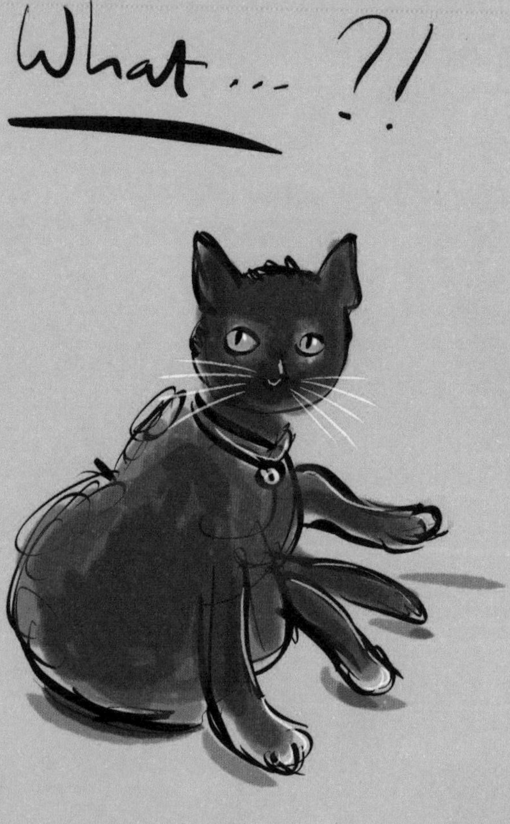
What ... ?!

"A cat is an animal who has more human feelings than any other being."

— Emily Brontë

"He is proud of the lustre of his coat, and cannot endure

that a hair of it should lie the wrong way."

— Champfleury

Chapter five.

Sleep.

"While we work, she rests and day dreams."

— agnès Varda

"They sleep
Sounder
than
we."

— Brian
Patten

"The cats sleep for days at a time and make love from the first star until dawn.

Their pleasures are fierce, and their sleep impenetrable."
— albert Camus

"Idleness exhausts
me completely."
— Arthur Conan Doyle

"Sleep is like a cat: it only comes to you if you ignore it." — Gillian Flynn

"Cats are connoisseurs of comfort."

—James Herriot

"The ideal of calm exists
in a sitting cat."
— Jules Renard

"a well-spent day brings happy sleep."

- Leonardo da Vinci

"Sleeping is my favourite thing, now I'm nineteen."

— Lily

"The trouble with sharing one's bed with cats is that they'd rather sleep

<u>on you</u> than beside you."
— Pam Brown

"Cats have it all —
admiration, an
endless sleep,
and company
only when
they
want
it."

— Rod McKuen

"as my cat would say, all hours are good for sleeping." —José Saramago

Tony and Missy,
When they were
both still quite small.

The last
bit.

"I think cats have a much better idea than we do of exactly what the world really is...

"They eat, they sleep, they choose who they love..

and bond loyally.

That's not a bad start."
— Peter Gethers

"When you are sorrowful
look again in your
heart, and you will
see that in truth you
are weeping for that
which
has
brought
you
delight."

- Kahlil Gibran

I think the idea is to make it up as you go along?
You see, we're just new and we don't really know yet
what we
ought
to be doing.

We're sure it's going to be fine.
Is there dinner yet?
When does all the fun start?

My sister here is the clever one. I'm a bit more worried about the life to come.

Paul lives in Manchester with Jeremy — and Panda. Also Bernard Socks.

Once upon a time we were lucky enough to have fester Cat living here, too.

<u>Thank you</u> to Jeremy and
all our friends. To my agent
Piers and my editor Anna
and all at HC. Special thanks
to everyone who volunteered
their cat friends for these
drawings :— (in no particular order)
Louise Spence + Princess Mollie

Marge Piercy + Zucchini Kitten

Johanna Mead + Pixel

Emma McCann + apple

Jenny Shirt + Marnie + Roo

Scott Lidell + Vinnie

Andrew + Mel Lawston + Buscemi

Helen Zwesdling + ambrose

Louise Whiddett + Yasmine
Cara Cooper + Wiggins
Vicki Forsyth + Cali + Bagheera
Anna Richardson-Freshney + Lucky
Ira Lightman + Missy
Debsi Ann Murphy + Bobbie Furmino
Fred Knitty + Bentley
Jessica Irving + Mitten
Nancy Tarallo + Jasper
Melissa Lapiere + Mudpie
Mark Irwin - Watson + Marilyn
Nix St + Winter
Katy Manning + Not my cat +
Not my Cat Either
Chris Hinchley + Jessie
John Freeman + Lily
Michael Goleniewski + Matilda
Anna Mwroiec + Parsons

ada Witch
Rob Blowers Spalding + Eric
Garry P. Flanagan + Jaime
Neil + Sue Perryman + Moriarty
Paul Driscoll + Sky + Ray-Ray
Ian Wheeler + Judi
Jackie Hagan + Stella
Brad Wolfe + Echo Blue
John McCullough + Flo
Townsend Shoulders + Tex
alison Drakes + Molly
Sile Martin + Ken
Laura Hnatiuk + Bruce
Menna Lukey + Ziggy + Maxi
Kate Mandalov + Blackie
Rosie anthony
Laura Niedbalski Mulcahy + Junior

Lloyd Nouvelle-Jones + Snuggles
Roger M. Dilley + Lady Squeeky
Sian Palmer
Jo Biza + Parker
Timothy Rodmell + Matilda
Sarah Perry + Kitten Mitten
Lois Fitzpatrick + Pepper, Charlie
                    + Salem
Linda Quick + Rosie
Stephen Selkie Woodhouse + Frankie
Judith Parker + Onion
Carole Hitchcox + Katya
Lee Fallows + Mr Cat
Nick Campbell
Bob Stone + Georgia Brown
Jo Lowes + Binky
Darren Ruddick + Newsha

Maddy Templeman + Rooster
Helen Dawson + Mouse
Jane Fallon + Pickle

Nicola Ingman + Keeley
Ian Harris + Fionn
Willow Funk + Leela
Simon Taylor + Nair, Orange +
Suzy Prince + Sonny   Dooby
Judy Le Pook + Arthur
Valerie Meiss
Yvette Hughes + Beans
Brendan Quinn + Tripod
Martin Williams + Binx
Cara Cooper + Wiggins
Ian Harris, Milly Johnson
+ Theo, Vince + Herman Crespo
Estelle Maher

Caroline + Nick Clarke +
Tony + Missy + Momo
Paul Anthony + Soxby
Jamie Griffiths + Ben
and of course our
Fester Cat and
Bernard Socks.

(and
anyone
else I
might
have left
out!)

SOURCES

Chapter One – Animal Nature

Charles Baudelaire, ('Les Chats', *Les Fleurs du mal,* 1857

Raymond Chandler (Quoted in *101 Amazing Things About Cat Lovers,* edited by Tod Hafer, 2016)

Jean Burden (*A Celebration of Cats,* 1974)

Jim Davis (Quoted in *Cat Secrets,* edited by Didier Hellepee, 2011)

H. P. Lovecraft ('The Rats in the Walls', 1923)

Lu You (*Selected Poems,* 1999)

Camille Paglia (*Sexual Personae,* 1990)

Rebecca West (*This Real Night,* 1985)

William Shakespeare (Falstaff in *Henry IV, Part 1,* 1597)

Ursula Andress (from *Inspirational Being,* edited by Cornelius D. Jones, 2012)

Chapter Two – Fun

Angela Carter (*The Bloody Chamber,* 1979)

Anthony Bourdain (*Kitchen Confidential,* 2000)

Miguel de Cervantes (*Don Quixote,* 1605)

Eleanor Farjeon (*The Little Bookroom,* 1965)

François Joseph Méry (Quoted in *The Tiger in the House* by Carl van Vechten, 1920)

Edward Gorey (Quoted in *The Strange Case of Edward Gorey* by Alexander Theroux, 2000)

Lilian Jackson Braun (*The Cat Who Went Underground*, 1989)

Garrison Keillor (Quoted in *The Quotable Cat Lover*, Charles Elliott, 2004)

Lloyd Alexander (*Time Cat*, 1963)

Rupert Brooke (*Delphi Complete Works of Rupert Brooke*, 2013)

Chapter Three – Friendship

Adam Rex (*Cold Cereal*, 2013)

Cleveland Amory (*The Cat Who Came for Christmas*, 1988)

Charles Bukowski ('My Cats' from *On Cats*, 2015)

Raymond Chandler (Letter to Hamish Hamilton, 1950)

Christopher Smart ('*Jubilate Agno*, Fragment B (For I will consider my Cat Jeoffry)', 1763)

Jean Cocteau (Quoted in *Of Cats and Men* by Sam Kalda, 2017)

Walter Lionel George (*A Bed of Roses*, 1911)

Ira Lightman (Quoted on Facebook, 2022)

Judith Kerr (From interview in the *Guardian* by Michelle Pauli, 2011)

Genki Kawamura (*If Cats Disappeared from the World*, 2012)

Kristen Cast (Quoted in *The Little Book for Cat Mums*, Charlie Ellis, 2021)

Mark Twain (Quoted in *Mark Twain for Cat Lovers*, Mark Dawidziak, 2016)

Jacquelyn Mitchard (Quoted in *Cats Are Special*, Kira Baum, 2007)

L. M. Montgomery (*Anne of the Island*, 1915)

Haruki Murakami (*What I Talk About When I Talk About Running*, 2009)

Nicholas Dodman (*Pets on the Couch*, 2017)

Charles Perrault ('Puss in Boots', 1697)

Percy Bysshe Shelley (*Quoted in Parasites, Pussycats and Psychosis* by E. Fuller Torrey, 2021)

Robertson Davies (Quoted in *Storms of Life*, Don Givens, 2008)

John Steinbeck (*The Winter of Our Discontent*, 1961)

Tay Hohoff (Quoted in *Chicken Soup for the Soul: My Clever, Curious, Caring Cat*, Amy Newmark, 2021)

Tom Cox (*Talk to the Tail*, 2011)

Colette (Quoted in *Chicken Soup for the Cat Lover's Soul* by Jack Canfield and Mark Victor Hansen, 2012)

Chapter Four – Philosophy

H. Allen Smith (*Rhubarb*, 1946)

William S. Burroughs (*The Cat Inside*, 1986)

Caroline Knapp (*Drinking: A Love Story*, 1996)

Colette (Quoted in *Cat Secrets*, Didier Hallepee, 2011)

Leonardo da Vinci (Quoted in *The Quotable Feline*, Jim Dratfield and Paul Coughlin, 2000)

Eckhart Tolle (*The Power of Now: A Guide to Spiritual Enlightenment*, 1997)

Erma Bombeck (Quoted in *Is There Tuna in Heaven?*, Kathy Finley, 2022)

Eugen Weber (Quoted in *Colette's Republic*, Patricia A. Tilburg, 2009)

Robert A. Heinlein (*Time Enough for Love*, 1973)

Helen Brown (*Cleo: How an Uppity Cat Helped Heal a Family*, 2009)

Ernest Hemingway (Quoted in *101 Amazing Things About Cat Lovers*, edited by Tod Hafer, 2016)

Irving Townsend (Quoted in *Good Mews: Inspirational Stories for Cat Lovers*, Kitty Chappell, 2010)

Jean Burden (Quoted in *Women Know Everything!*, Karen Weekes, 2011)

Jerome K. Jerome (Quoted in *In the Company of Cats*, British Library, 2014)

John N. Gray (*Feline Philosophy: Cats and the Meaning of Life*, 2020)

Jules Verne (Quoted in *Chicken Soup for the Soul: The Cat Really Did That?*, Amy Newmark, 2017)

Laini Taylor (*Night of Cake and Puppets*, 2013)

Doris Lessing (*On Cats*, 1967)

Lewis Carroll (*Alice's Adventures in Wonderland*, 1865)

Theresa Mancuso (*Cats Do It Better Than People*, 2004)

Marge Piercy (Quoted on Facebook, 2022)

Nicola Griffith (*Hild*, 2014)

Edgar Allan Poe (Quoted in *Edgar Allan Poe: His Words*, Daniel Coenn, 2014)

Rai Aren (*Revelation of the Sands*, 2015)

Judith Merkle Riley (Quoted in *Why Don't Cats Go Bald?* by Skip Sullivan and David Fisher, 2008)

Muriel Spark (*A Far Cry from Kensington*, 1988)

Walter Scott (*Our Dumb Friends; Or Conversations of a Father with his Children, about Dogs, Horses, Donkeys and Cats*, Thomas Jackson, 1865)

Emily Brontë ('The Cat', 1842)

Champleury (*Les chats: Histoire, mœurs observations, anecdotes*, 1869)

Chapter Five – Sleep

Agnès Varda (Short film, *Hommage à Zgougou*, 2014)

Brian Patten (From 'Inessential Things' in *Selected Poems*, 2007)

Albert Camus (*A Happy Death*, 1971)

Arthur Conan Doyle (*The Sign of Four*, 1890)

Gillian Flynn (*Gone Girl*, 2012)

James Herriot (*James Herriot's Cat Stories*, 1994)

Jules Renard (Quoted in *Meow: A Book of Happiness for Cat Lovers*, Anouska Jones, 2015)

Leonardo da Vinci (Quoted in *Success Mantras: by Leonardo da Vinci*, Uttam Ghosh, 2021)

Pam Brown (Quoted in *Cats Don't Always Land on Their Feet*, Erin Barrett and Jack Mingo, 2002)

Rod McKuen (*Rod McKuen's Book of Days and a Month of Sundays*, 1980)

José Saramago (*Seeing*, 2004)

Peter Gethers (*Forever Norton: The Perfect Cat, His Flawed Human and Life's Greatest Lesson*, 2010)

Kahlil Gibran (*The Prophet*, 1923)